Praying Mantis

Ultimate Care Guide

Keep Them Happy and Healthy
Praying Mantis Step by Step
Pet Care Guide

By Thomas Green

Foreword

For many people, myself included, the idea of keeping insects as pets did not come naturally. As a child, I was not a fan of insects. After an addition was built onto our home, the warmth of the first winter fire hatched out thousands of katydids or bush crickets that were indigenous to the area.

A form of grasshopper, katydids have very long legs and antennae, and are superb jumpers. I was convinced that the creatures nursed a particular vendetta against me.

At night after I turned out the light, I would hear one or more hopping or crawling around my room. There was no sleeping with that going on, and I was forced to do battle with the little beasts night after night.

No one who knew me then would ever imagine that I would cultivate an interest in insects. Praying mantids are, however, unlike any other insect, which is why one of the first and most comprehensive books on their care, by Orin McMonigle, was called *Keeping Aliens*.

My feeling about insects began to loosen up when I took up photography and spent many happy hours photographing bees feeding on a honeysuckle bush. My grandmother had always counseled, "They'll leave you alone if you leave them alone."

The advice proved to be true. I didn't get any stings, but I did get a series of fascinating photos that let me see a bee's "face" for the first time. From there, I spent many years getting close-ups of butterflies for the same reason.

During one of those outings, I took a picture of a praying mantis by accident. It was a female *Mantis religiosa*, or European Mantis, the ubiquitous green creature whose image comes to mind when we think "praying mantis."

The mantid's vibrant green body blended in so beautifully with the grass, I didn't see it until I looked at the pictures later. There, staring back at me, was the distinctive triangular head and large green eyes that did indeed look "alien."

There was, however, something oddly intelligent and benign about the creature's expression. I started looking for more mantids to photograph, and began to learn about these fascinating creatures in greater detail. It was then that I discovered their popularity among hobbyists.

While my own efforts at keeping mantids have been minimal compared to hardcore enthusiasts, I can say, with great conviction that mantids make excellent pets.

They are clean and require a minimal amount of space. They do not carry disease. No species is poisonous, and they rarely bite. When they do, it's far less painful than a pin prick. In fact, you may not notice it at all.

There is a necessity to feed mantids live prey insects, which can be a little "icky" for people who have a "thing" about your average run of the mill "bug." I solved this by buying my feeder insects in bags at a big box pet store and just dumping them in the feeding holes in the containers in which my mantids lived.

The following text was born of my desire to provide a somewhat more accessible overview of mantid care for anyone contemplating keeping these creatures as companions.

Without a doubt, the definitive work on the subject is Orin McMonigle's *Keeping the Praying Mantis*, but like many encyclopedic works, it can be daunting for someone just thinking about taking up the hobby.

My goal here is to provide you with a primer on mantids and mantid care to help you decide if this is a good hobby to pursue. I commend to you both McMonigle's work and the many excellent resources you will find online to help you perfect your own husbandry skills.

I, for one, am very glad that stray *Mantis religiosa* wandered into my photograph that day. Overcoming my revulsion and even fear of insects has allowed me to understand that there is a vast and complicated "world" within our bigger human sphere of affairs.

In that world, there are mighty hunters like the mantis, and smaller creatures destined to be its prey. It is a place filled with social order and ritual, complicated "displays" to communicate messages, and epic tragedy — as when a female mantis turns around and bites off the head of her suitor.

Without question, this microcosm is endlessly fascinated and in that realm, the praying mantis is a lordly figure among its fellow insects.

Table of Contents

Table of Contents

Table of Contents

Table of Contents

Chapter 1 –Introduction to Praying Mantids

The order of insects that includes praying mantids is "mantodea." It's a huge group, with more than 2,400 species! These fascinating creatures are found around the world in a variety of environmental circumstances.

(Before we proceed, let me make a point about clarifying language. "Mantis" is undeniably singular, but the plural a bit more difficult. In recent years, "mantid" has come into use as both a singular and plural form. You will see all used in this text, hopefully without too much confusion!)

Common Perceptions

The ubiquitous image that springs to mind when you hear the phrase "praying mantis" is a bright green insect with a triangular head and a long, narrow body.

In truth, mantids come in an array of shapes and colors, all beautifully suited to blend into their native environments. Mantids are superb masters of camouflage, both as a matter of survival and as a hunting adaptation.

The name "praying mantis" derives from the manner in which the insect holds its forelegs, as if in an attitude of prayer. There are many legends about this characteristic of mantids, including the belief in some Muslim cultures that a mantis always points the way to Mecca.

While that is a lovely and reverential idea, those limbs are not as benign as the nomenclature suggests. Praying mantids are carnivorous hunters that are very, very good at what they do.

Many people confuse praying mantids with the similar "walking stick" insects that are phasmids. The major difference is that the walking sticks are plant eaters or herbivores.

Physical Characteristics and Biology

Like most insects, mantids develop through discernible life stages, in this instance, egg, nymph, and adult. Because the immature nymph looks like what it is — a miniature adult — it does not have a distinct name.

Vision

Praying mantids have large, compound eyes that afford them excellent vision. When viewed in close-up through the wonders of macro photography, mantids' eyes are one of their most beautiful features.

The "shopping" list of mantid visual abilities is incredibly impressive:

- compound eyes with a 300 degree field of vision
- stereoscopic, binocular vision
- capability for triangulation
- perception of parallax

Using the compound eyes to their full advantage, a mantis can distinguish color, shape, and movement — necessary skills in the life of a highly efficient hunter.

Mantid vision is, in fact, stereoscopic. They can accurately judge distance and have a 300 degree field of vision coupled with the ability to swivel their heads nearly 8 degrees.

The praying mantis also possesses the ability to use parallax. This means that mantids are able to distinguish the movement of an object against a more distant background, which is, essentially, depth perception.

This reinforces their binocular ability to triangulate the position of their prey. Very little escapes the attention of a praying mantis, which makes vision absolutely essential to their survival.

Limited Night Vision

Because of their heavy reliance on vision, there are no cave-dwelling mantids. The creatures will eat at night, but only when prey basically runs right into them.

However, as the light diminishes each day, the eyes of many species do turn dark in order to absorb more available light, returning to normal the next day.

Neither the color change nor the massive size of the eyes in relation to the head and body equate with superior night time vision, though. If a mantid's eyes are completely obscured, it will starve to death.

Presence of a Pseudopupil

When you look at a mantis, you will see that its head moves, following your motion. This air of attention is emphasized by the dark spot in each compound eye called a pseudopupil.

This spot is only an optical illusion, however, created by the way light is refracted within the multi-faceted compound eye.

Depending on the position of the mantis, the spot will change size, but this is not due to the contraction of a real pupil as is seen in humans.

The entire surface of the eye will change color in relation to ambient light, sometimes appearing almost tan in bright sunlight.

Femoral Brush

A patch on the inside of the leg called the femoral brush is used by the mantis expressly to keep the surface of the eye clean. This action does not, in any way, harm the surface of the eye, and is a routine part of the fastidious mantis' daily self-care.

Ocelli

In truth, however, mantids have five eyes, the two that are clearly prominent and distinguishable upon examination, and three simple eyes.

These "ocelli" sit between the antennae in a triangular formation and help the mantis distinguish between light and dark.

Using all five eyes in concert, a mantis has the potential to spot prey at a distance of up to 60 feet / 18.3 meters and to view the world in a wide range of wavelengths, including ultraviolet light.

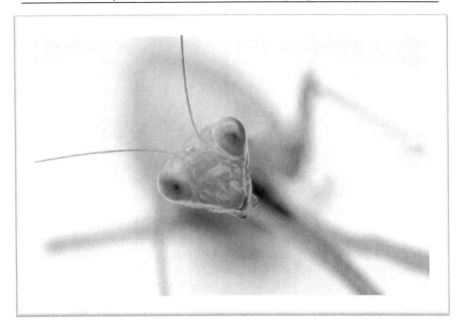

Forelegs

The forelegs of a mantis are raptorial in nature and as integral to their hunting prowess as their compound eyes. These appendages are outfitted with a series of sharp spines and fold upward to form a trap for unsuspecting victims.

The upper portion of the leg that attaches to the "shoulder" is called the coxa. Moving down the leg, the first joint is the trochanter, which connects to the femur, which in turn leads to the tibia, and finally the tarsus.

There are four hind legs that play no role in hunting. These walking legs do, however, create a stable platform for the creature. Without that base, the armored forelegs would be useless.

In addition, the "feet" of a mantis are outfitted with adhesive pads called euplantulae that allow the creatures to walk up smooth surfaces as if gravity did not exist.

If, in captivity, there is a need to keep mantids from using this adaptation, a fine coating of petroleum jelly will destroy their ability to sustain traction.

Smell and Taste

The antennae of a mantis function as its major olfactory organ. This means the mantis may smell the prey itself, or items like rotting plant and animal material to which the insects are attracted.

Mantid's mouths are outfitted with two sensory "palps" with which they taste their food. The palps guide the mantis in feeding and may also have a secondary odor distinguishing ability.

The interaction of these two sensory systems suggests that a mantis can "taste" smells.

Hearing

A mantis has only one ear, which is located under the body and right at the base of the back legs. There, a deep and narrow groove holds two tympanic membranes.

(Note that this physical feature is often absent or greatly diminished in flightless females and some neotropical species.)

Circulation and Breathing

The circulation of blood through the body's system is open and is not related to the action of the respiratory system. It's perfectly possible for a mantis that is missing a limb to survive for days regardless of how much blood it has lost.

Breathing occurs through a series of openings called spiracles from which tubes or trachea branch out. This is a passive process and is not dependent on any single organ.

This system, although simple, can be very limited. Some species will fall over dead if they do not have access to sufficient air flow. Also, if an insect's body becomes coated in some thick substance that blocks the spiracles, asphyxiation will occur fairly quickly.

Although mantids do not breathe in the sense that we do, you may see large, engorged females contracting their abdominal muscles in a rhythmic pattern to increase the flow of air over their spiracles.

Digestion and Elimination

Mantids eat all of their prey. What is not digestible is excreted through openings called the malpighian tubules as dry pellets along with crystallized uric acid.

Mantids do drink regularly, which is somewhat unusual among arthropods. Their system requires that the moisture lost during respiration be replaced and the liquid helps to flush the uric acid from their system.

Wings

The forewings of a mantis are called tegmina. They both hide and protect the bigger hind wings, which are visibly membranous and sit folded beneath the tegmina.

Typically the tegmina, which serve as protection for the abdomen, play a key role in the mantid's camouflage abilities. It is rare for these wings to be of a contrasting color to the body.

Although both males and females have wings, generally they are only used for flight by males. Females eat too much and rapidly become too large.

Exoskeleton and Molting

The exoskeleton or outer body covering of a mantis is made of chitin. While portions of the abdomen can stretch, the exoskeleton cannot, necessitating a progression of molts (shedding of the skin) to allow the mantis to grow.

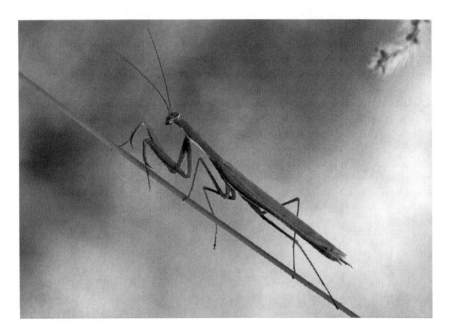

Molting takes from 5-20 minutes. During the process, the mantis completely removes its body from the old covering or exoskeleton and then spends an hour inflating into its new exoskeleton.

Unlike some insects, mantids do not eat their cast-off exoskeleton. From nymph to adult, a mantid will molt 6-9 times.

Powers of Regeneration

If a mantis nymph loses a walking limb, the limb regenerates and is fully functional after the next molt. This process is not as efficient for the raptorial front legs which, if damaged, may require several molts to regain functionality.

Depending on the nature of a break or injury, however, the damage may cause the molting process to go wrong and no repair occurs, which is a leading cause of death in developing mantids.

Camouflage

Mantid's ability to appear invisible against a given background is called "crypsis." This adaptation may be a tactic to avoid being eaten by a larger predator, an aid in securing prey, or both.

Many species evolve to mimic the appearance of dead leaves, while others have developed colorations and appendages that look like bright green leaves, lichen, bark, twigs, grass, or flowers.

Additionally, most mantids can change their body color slightly to more accurately conceal themselves. This is not as rapid as the change that may be seen in some lizards, and the ability may only be present just after a molt.

Other species clearly exhibit the ability to recognize color, and will position themselves accordingly for maximum concealment.

Reproduction

Most species of mantis exhibit sexual cannibalism, with the female biting off the head of the male. This is typically avoided in captive species by making sure that the female is well fed before mating, and by quickly removing the male from the breeding box as soon as possible.

In mating, the male leaps onto the back of the female, holding onto her thorax with his forelegs. The female will deposit anywhere from 10 to 400 eggs depending on the species.

Egg Sacs or Oothecae

She excretes her eggs from abdominal glands in a mass of froth that hardens into a protective casing called an ootheca. This may be attached to a flat surface, or affixed to adjacent plant matter. Some species will even deposit their "egg sacs" on the ground.

An ability to recognize the ootheca of popular mantid species is a good one for enthusiasts to cultivate. One of the draws of keeping mantids as a hobby is the option to gather specimens in the wild. It is often much easier to locate the ootheca and to allow it to hatch than it is to attempt to capture adult mantis specimens.

Mantids and Mankind

When not kept as pets, the primary relationship mantids share with humans involves pest control. Praying mantids are routinely released by gardeners and farmers to dispatch with nuisance insects.

In fact, many of the mantids that are now most common in the United States were originally imported from Asia and Europe for this very reason. Their effectiveness at this "job" is nothing short of legendary.

Options for Release

This fact is of considerable benefit to the hobbyist. Many people who keep exotic pets, for instance various species of frogs, do not have the option of releasing their pets in the wild.

As an example, the African Clawed Frog, which has been popular among amphibian keepers for the past 20 years, is a highly predatory species.

Escapees, and pets that have been released, have not only been responsible for the decimation of local populations, but also for the spread of the deadly disease chytrid.

When you purchase mantid species or capture wild specimen, you can choose to concentrate on native and adventive (introduced and now common) species.

This means that when you hatch out more nymphs than you can possibly tend, the excess population does not have to be destroyed, and can simply be set free.

Mantids and Gardening

If you are both a gardener and a mantid keeper, you have a near perfect combination of avocations. Most hobbyists do not want to destroy mantids in their care for any reason other than humane concerns often after a bad molt, so the option for release is especially attractive.

It is critical, however, that you pay attention to the release status of any species you buy. Many exotics can now be obtained from online sources and are not suitable for release outside their native range.

If you plan on keeping exotic species and must discontinue your hobby for any reason, you will need a way to either relocate or euthanize your population.

Enthusiast discussion groups online often make it possible for mantids to be placed with new keepers rather than destroyed. If euthanasia does become necessary, placing the mantid in the freezer is generally considered to be the most humane method.

Although such considerations may seem unpleasant to people who are just considering entering the hobby, responsible mantid care, especially in relation to release procedures is essential.

The Mantid Hobby

There is no question that the practice of keeping mantids as pets is a small and very specialized hobby. There has been growing interest in recent years, however, in having "mini beasts."

Insects make attractive pets due to their low cost, minimal housing requirements, and low maintenance needs.

The Internet has proved to be an invaluable resource to allow hobbyists to contact one another and exchange information and often "livestock."

Authoritative Resources

The oldest and most authoritative online enthusiast community is The Mantid Forum at MantidForum.net. This is an excellent site to meet other mantis keepers and to learn from their successes and failures.

The exhaustive and definitive published work on the subject is *Keeping the Praying Mantis* by Orin McMonigle, an encyclopedic examination of all that is involved in the husbandry of mantid species.

The "Throw-Away Pet" Notion

This text is heavily indebted to McMonigle's work, but has a different purpose in mind — helping you to make a decision. I strongly object to any notion of a "throw-away" pet, including insects.

Praying mantids, although they survive just a few months, are living creatures deserving of the same level of care to which any "pet" is entitled.

My goal is to offer to you an introduction to the keeping of mantids as a hobby with the clear caveat that this is the kind of hobby you can happily cultivate and hone for years.

The longer you keep mantids, the more you will learn about them. You will develop your own "tricks" for successful breeding, and you will have your own share of stellar triumphs and disasters.

The good thing is that you can begin by collecting mantids in the wild and, for little if any investment, find out if this bug will bite you.

(Not literally. Certainly mantids can bite, but only the really big ones will ever make you feel as if you've been pinched, and none are poisonous or even carry diseases.)

Mantids and Children

Keeping praying mantids meshes well with educational projects both in traditional classrooms and home school environments. The minimal financial outlay for livestock and equipment makes the prospect highly attractive in a budgetary sense.

Certainly, mantid husbandry is a ripe field for lessons in insect behavior and can encompass a project following the life cycle of the creatures from egg to fully grown adult.

Younger children might require help tending mantids, especially in regard to temperature, humidity, and feeding, but after the age of 12, any youngster should be able to care for the insects on their own.

Remember, however, that these insects are carnivorous and cannibalistic. They must be fed live prey. Younger, more sensitive and impressionable children may find this highly disturbing.

Make sure that all factors of mantid care have been fully explained to children before the creatures are brought into the home or classroom.

Also, the students should understand the short lifespan of mantids, and the potential need for euthanasia if a molt goes wrong.

There is very little about keeping mantids that sugar coats the hard realities of life, but that does not negate the rewards of keeping company with these fascinating insects.

Just make sure that children are fully prepared for all aspects of the project before proceeding.

Collecting Mantids in the Wild

You will have the greatest luck finding mantids in the wild from mid- to late summer. Early in the season tiny nymphs are out there, but they're hard to locate and easily damaged when caught in nets.

On sunny days, the larger species are generally profuse in meadows or gardens and are captured by sweeping the vegetation with a net. Because of their greater size, they are less likely to be injured in this fashion.

At night, flying species are attracted to lights in just about any setting including gas stations and strip malls. These individuals can simply be picked up off the surface on which they're sitting and placed in a container for transport.

Note that in some species of flying mantids, only the males are actually capable of flight, so females would have to be found in adjacent fields if your intent is to breed the species in captivity.

Locating Oothecae

Often it's easier to find oothecae in the wild and to allow them to hatch in captivity than it is to catch a mantis. In the autumn, the foamy looking egg sacks are clearly visible after the leaves have fallen from the trees.

Look on low hanging branches, as well as on rocks and other structures about 12 in / 30.48 cm off the ground near buildings.

Removing Oothecae

Be extremely careful about removing oothecae from surfaces to which they have been attached. If the ootheca is on a branch, take the whole limb rather than trying to cut away the delicate egg sack.

If you have no choice but to try to remove the ootheca, use a razor blade. Work slowly and carefully, trying not to expose any of the eggs inside to the elements.

Even if the outer casing is damaged, however, the bulk of the eggs in the ootheca should still hatch. In general, my best advice is not to give up on any oothecae. They'll often hatch when you least expect them to!

I'll discuss handling oothecae later in this book, but it's important to orient the egg sac appropriately when you store it for hatching so the nymphs can successfully emerge.

Generally the structure of the oothecae will help you to determine "front" and "back," but taking a digital photograph as a reference prior to collection is a good idea.

This will also help you to learn the oothecae of individual species, and to go back to prime locations in subsequent seasons to harvest more egg sacs.

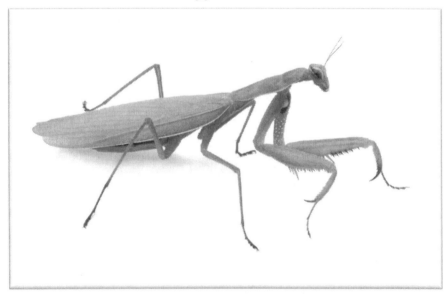

Pros and Cons of Keeping Praying Mantids

While many people might balk at the idea of having an insect as a pet, praying mantids have advantages for people with limited space and time to devote to a companion.

While it might be true that you aren't going to walk your mantid like a dog, you may be surprised at what an engrossing part of your life they can become. You may even find that you become rather attached to your pets.

To some extent, mantids do interact with their keepers. Hobbyists say their mantids follow their movements, and many are highly receptive to being hand fed.

Pros of Keeping Mantids

Although a room full of enthusiasts could likely come up with many more "positives" about their hobby, these are, to my mind, the major points in favor of becoming a "manticulturist."

- Mantids are surprisingly friendly.

They are not aggressive insects towards humans and only the largest specimens can bite hard enough for you to feel more than the slightest pinch.

Very occasionally you may lose a tiny dot of blood, but you're not facing the prospect of serious injury.

- *Most mantids don't mind being handled.*

Once you get over the "ick" factor that many people experience initially with insects, you may find you enjoy how easily a mantid reacts to human interaction.

- *These insects do not carry any disease, and they are neat and clean.*

You will spend only a minimal amount of time on maintenance. In fact, the only real reason to clean the habitat is a matter of aesthetics, which is your concern, not the mantid's.

- *There is not one species of poisonous praying mantis.*

This is certainly not a statement that can be made about most potential companion insects.

- *Getting started is not an expensive proposition.*

This being said, it is very easy to get carried away the longer you stay with the hobby. It's all too common to be consumed by the collector mentality.

- *Enthusiasts are free to keep native and naturalized species.*

Importing specimens is regulated in most countries, but you can walk right out in your backyard and probably find a mantis to keep as a pet. Exotic species are available, but must not be released into the wild.

(This is not only to protect the native species, but to ensure that the hobby of keeping any kind of insect does not become subject to more stringent regulation due to the irresponsible actions of a few people.)

Cons of Keeping Mantids

Describing the "cons" of praying mantis ownership is a bit more difficult. The one that comes to mind immediately is that you may face problems locating all the species you'd like to keep.

Some imports are illegal, but there are dozens of captive bred species that are easily obtained. As long as you are happy with those mantids, you will have more than enough to keep you busy.

Sometimes, however, mantid keepers become consumed by the "collector" mentality. You will find yourself setting goals, "I want to have this species or that species" in my collection, or "I want to successfully raise this mantid."

That is only a "con" if you regard the process as a frustration rather than a challenge. Most stamp collectors, for instance, *want* to find that elusive stamp, but may well derive as much pleasure from the search as the acquisition.

Beyond that potential negative, you may find that other members of your household are not receptive to living with "bugs," a reaction that generally wears off as they get to know your mantids.

Basically, if you have an interest in keeping interesting, low maintenance insects like mantids, there really aren't that many negatives involved!

Buying Mantids

While it is perfectly reasonable to assume that you can acquire your mantids in your own backyard or someplace nearby – in a park or a rural setting – many beginners choose to purchase their first specimens.

The following prices were accurate and the species were available in the pet trade at the time of this writing, early in 2014.

(All prices cited are for adult mantids. Nymphs and oothecae are both available from supply houses and enthusiasts.)

Note that pricing will vary widely by vendor and availability, which is often seasonal. It is quite common for species to pass in and out of the hobby, so there is no way to determine a set list of available mantids at any given time although some perennial favorites show up routinely, like *Mantis religiosa*.

(Most of these species are profiled in the following two chapters on mantids found in the United States, as well as those species that are considered rare or exotic.)

Price Range $12 - $15 / £7 - £9

Oxypilus distinctus
Bolbena hottentotta
Acromantis farmosa
Acromantis magna
Hierodula bipapilla
Miomantis paykullii
Odontomantis planiceps
Orthodera novaezealandiae
Polyspilota aeruginosa
Sinomantis denticulata
Sphodromantis centralis
Statilia maculata
Statilia parva
Statilia nemoralis
Creobroter gemmatus
Creobroter pictipennis
Didymocorypha lanceolata
Sphodromantis lineola
Creobroter apicalis
Hierodula multispina
Mantis religiosa
Pseudoharpax virescen
Stagmomantis carolina
Brunneria borealis
Gonatista grisea

Hierodula patellifera patellifera
Leptomentella sp.
Omomantis zebrata
Sphodromantis viridis
Tenodera angustipennis

Price Range $15 - $30 / £9 - £18

Ephestiasula pictipes
Parasphendale affinis
Parasphendale agrionina
Sphodromantis gastrica
Hierodula keralensis
Hierodula membranacea
Hierodula unimaculata
Hagiotata hofmanni
Hierodula majuscula
Idolomorpha lateralis
Mesopteryx alata
Nilomantis flower
Pnigomantis medioconstricta
Popa spurca
Sphodropoda quinquedens
Phyllocrania paradoxa
Pseudocreobotra ocellata
Rhombodera basalis
Cilnia humeralis
Cerotomantis sausurii
Phylothellys werneri
Pseudocreobotra wahlbergii
Caliris elegans

Euchomenella macrops
Archimantis latistyla
Pseudempusa pinnapavonis

Price Range $30 - $50 / £18 - £30

Empusa pennata
Blepharopsis mendica
Deroplatys desiccata
Deroplatys lobata
Gongylus gongylodes
Hymenopus coronatus
Idolomantis
Parymenopus davisoni

This is certainly not an exhaustive list of all the mantid species that might be available online at any one time.

It is also possible to acquire specimens through enthusiast communities and discussion groups, although this venue might be trade or barter situation over an actual purchase.

Any time that you join a discussion community, do not simply jump in. Spend time "lurking" to learn the etiquette of the given group.

Many forums have rules against members selling live mantids and associated paraphernalia, but do encourage the adopting out of excess livestock over euthanasia.

Chapter 2 - Mantid Species - United States

There are 28 species of mantids currently present in the United States. Many of these specimens are non-native species that were introduced in the late 19th and early 20th centuries by gardeners and enthusiasts. Those introduced species are now considered to be "adventive" or naturalized and are, for all practical purposes, natives.

Nine of the 28 species are rarely kept by hobbyists either because they are rare or because they do not adapt well in captivity. These species are:

- *Tithrone clauseni*
- *Tithrone corseuili*
- *Mantoida maya*
- *Bactromantis virga*
- *Oligonicella bolliana*
- *Litaneutria borealis*
- *Litaneutria longipennis*
- *Stagmomantis gracilipes*
- *Stagmomantis montana*

The remaining species in the U.S. are all options to be kept by enthusiasts, although not all are easily raised in captivity.

The following descriptions are meant as a brief introduction to various mantids. Remember, there are more than 2,400 species of these insects!

Scudder Mantis (*Oligonicella scudderi*)

Scudder's Mantis is one of the smallest species found in the United States at just 1 - 1 1/3 in / approx. 2.54 cm in length. Long, delicate, brown and tan stripes run the length of their bodies, and when viewed in magnification, they have two distinct bumps behind the eyes.

This species is found in a range from Nebraska to Florida.

Slim Mexican Mantis (*Bactromantis Mexicana*)

The Slim Mexican Mantis is very similar in appearance to Scudder's Mantis but is somewhat longer. This species can be located from Arizona south into Central America.

Grass Mantis (*Thesprotia graminis*)

The Grass Mantis is quite dainty and lives a well-camouflaged existence in fields and near stands of pine trees. Only males of this species have wings that are kept tightly folded against the body.

The species is popular with enthusiasts because they can be kept in communities with almost no instances of cannibalism. Females reach a maximum size of 2 in / 5.08 cm. The Grass Mantis can be found in a range from Georgia to Texas and south into Mexico.

Mediterranean Mantis (*Iris oratoria*)

The Mediterranean Mantis was introduced in California in 1933 and can now be found across most of the American Southwest including Arizona, Nevada, New Mexico and Texas.

The hind wings are marked with a distinctive black eyespot. Adults are about 0.25-0.75 in / 0.64 – 1.9 cm in length. The Mediterranean Mantis closely resembles the various species of *Stagmomantis* indigenous to the United States.

Grizzled Bark Mantis (*Gonatista grisea*)

The Grizzled Bark Mantis has evolved to match lichen present on tree bark. They are a fast-moving species, darting about on tree trunks with motions that closely mimic the motion of crabs.

Adults range in size from 1 1/3 to 1 2/3 in / 3.4 – 4.2 cm in length and are broad and flat in shape. When they press themselves against tree bark, the Grizzled Bark Mantis essentially disappears.

The species is found in the southeastern United States as far north as North Carolina, with some specimens showing up periodically in Florida.

Brunner's Mantis (*Brunneria borealis*)

Brunner's Mantis displays variable abdominal strips in green, yellow, and red. Wild specimens have a green base color, while those raised in captivity are pink.

Often called the "stick mantis," it lives in tall grass and looks so much like the adjacent stems, the creature is very hard to pick out.

This species is unique in that they have a single gender only. The females reproduce via parthenogenesis. Their eggs develop without fertilization.

Brunner's Mantis is found in the southern United States from Texas into Florida and North Carolina, and has been naturalized in Hawaii.

Minor Ground Mantis (*Litaneutria minor*)

As adults, the Minor Ground Mantis is about 1.3 in / 3.3 cm in length. They favor dry areas of scrub brush in a long range from British Columbia south to Mexico. Females of the species can display a wide variety of patterns and colors.

In captivity, the Minor Ground Mantis is incapable of climbing glass surfaces, and will place their oothecae low in the cage unless they're given a way to climb to the screen lid of their enclosure.

Obscure Ground Mantis (*Litaneutria obscure*)

The Obscure Ground Mantis is just slightly smaller than the Minor Ground Mantis at 1.3 in / 3.3 cm and is found primarily in California, but also ranging into Arizona, New Mexico, and Texas.

Their oothecae are quite small and black, containing only a couple of dozen eggs. As the name implies, this species stays primarily on the ground or in the lower level of their habitat if kept in captivity.

They are agile and quick, and should be fed small arthropods that they can easily overcome. The Obscure Ground Mantis is rare in the hobby.

European Mantis (*Mantis religiosa*)

The European Mantis is the second most common of the North American mantid species and has the honor of being the official Connecticut state insect.

The species sports a black-encircled yellow eyespot on the inside of each foreleg, although in some individuals the same area can be dark blue instead.

There are eight sub-species of the European Mantis found in Europe and in the tropics, making it one of the most accessible species for enthusiasts in those areas.

Females European Mantids average 2.5 in / 6.4 cm in length.

Texas Unicorn Mantis (*Phyllovates chlorophaea*)

A large, bulky, and handsome species, female Texas Unicorn Mantids can reach a length of more than 2.75 in / 6.99 cm.

A popular species kept by enthusiasts, most of the captive bred specimens can be traced to a female captured in Brownsville, Texas in 2007.

Due to the wide range of this species, which extends into South America, you may see it listed as the Mexican, Central, and South American Unicorn Mantis.

Arizona Unicorn Mantis (*Pseudovates arizonae*)

A bright green, exotic looking mantis with distinctive brown spots, the Arizona Unicorn Mantis is a beautiful specimen, popular with hobbyists. Its large horn is composed of two sections and rises from the center of the forehead.

Although prized for its appearance, the species is difficult to raise. Nymphs hatch and survive well, but males are slow to mature and do not show much interest in mating with females. In the wild, only a single generation is born per year. This mantis is found in Arizona only.

California Mantis (*Stagmomantis californica*)

Female California Mantids have a line of yellow running along the top of their hind wings. When the wings are raised, there are four dark bands present on the dorsal abdomen.

In addition to California, the species is found in Colorado, New Mexico, and Texas.

Carolina Mantis (*Stagmomantis carolina*)

The Carolina Mantis is the most common mantis in the
United States, reaching an average length of 2.25 in / 5.71
cm. It is highly variable, with specimens seen in shades of
green, mottled gray, brown, yellow, tan, black, and pink.

Over the years, this degree of variation has led to the
attachment of 43 different names to the species. The dark
hind wings are almost black, with an orange to brown
coloration at the base and top. In males, the wings are
sometimes a deep blue.

The species is quite easy to keep, although adult females
are especially voracious. The species ranges in a northern
band from New Jersey to Utah and south into Central
America.

Larger Florida Mantis (*Stagmomantis floridensis*)

The female Larger Florida Mantis can grow to more than
3.5 in / 8.9 cm in length. Their wings have a yellow
checkered pattern.

The wings are shorter in relation to the body than the very
similar Carolina Mantis. The Larger Florida Mantis,
however, is found only in the state of Florida.

Bordered Mantis (*Stagmomantis limbata*)

A very common species in the American Southwest, the Bordered Mantis has a bulky body. Females have bright yellow hind wings with a checkered pattern of clear "windows."

This is also an easily kept species, although the nymphs are highly cannibalistic. The Bordered Mantis can be found easily in California, Arizona, and Texas and also ranges into Mexico.

Narrow-Winged Mantis (*Tenodora angustipennis*)

A slim mantis that grows to a length of 3 in / 8 cm, the adult Narrow-Winged Mantis sports a vivid orange spot between the forelegs. The transparent hind wings are a pale pink to tan.

Specimens of this species are found throughout the United States, but are more typical from Pennsylvania south into Georgia and the surrounding area.

Chinese Mantis (*Tenodera sinensis*)

The largest species in the United States, the Chinese Mantis reaches a maximum length of 4 in / 10 cm. It is very common in the eastern and central parts of the country and is easily identified by the colorful vertical ridges on the face.

The hind wings are black, and there is a distinctive spot of pale yellow behind the forelegs. Both males and females are capable of flight, although females are generally too heavy to do so.

Yersin's Ground Mantis (*Yersiniops sophronicum*)

Although inconspicuous as a species, Yersin's Ground Mantis has prominent conical eyes. They are curious and inquisitive by nature, and quite active. Their coloration ranges from tan to brown. Adults reach a maximum size of 0.5 in / 1.3 cm.

Long hind legs and a good ability to jump (and run) have led to the species sometimes being called a "Grasshopper Mantis." Yersin's Ground Mantis is found throughout the American Southwest, but not in California.

Horned Ground Mantis (*Yersiniops solitarium*)

The Horned Ground Mantis is closely related to Yersin's Ground Mantis and has a similar appearance, although it can reach 1.0 in / 2.5 cm in length and has more widely spaced eyes. The range for the two species is identical in the American Southwest excluding California.

Chapter 3 – Selected World Species

The following are a sampling of some species of mantids found around the world, including some that are rare and exotic. While many are desirable in the hobby, not all are readily available for purchase or trade.

Venezuelan Deadleaf Mantis (*Acanthops falcata*)

A distinguishing trait of the Venezuelan Deadleaf Mantis is its ability to fold its front legs into a scoop. Females reach a maximum length of 2 in / 5 cm.

They are capable of making an impressive threat display by exposing vibrant black, yellow, and purple abdominal markings. The species is native to Venezuela, the northern regions of South America, and Mexico.

Acromantis spp.

Acromantis mantids are small, with a very "standard" appearance. They are not equipped with any special adaptations that allow them to mimic flowers.

Males are less than one inch in length, while females will be 1.25 in / 3.18 cm.

There are 21 species in this group distributed across Southeast Asia. Three species, including *Acromantis farmosa* and *Acromantis magna* are kept by hobbyists.

Cameroon Mantis (*Alalomantis muta*)

The inside of the Cameroon Mantis' femurs are marked with large, white circles edged in black. Adults reach a maximum size of 3.0 in / 7.6 cm.

Both nymphs and adults feed ravenously. The species is found in Cameroon east to Uganda.

Australian Giant Mantis (*Archimantis sp.*)

The Australian Giant Mantis grows to a maximum length of 4 in / 10 cm, but captive specimens tend to be smaller. Altogether, there are nine species in this group and, where available, are popular with enthusiasts for their large size. They are found throughout Australia.

Creobroter

The Creobroter mantids are flower mantids. They are vivid and varicolored specimens, seen in shades of white, red, yellow, and brown, often with striking patterns.

Common to Western Asia, these mantids grow to be 1 – 2 in / 3-5 cm in length by gender, with males being the smaller individuals.

Lesser Devil's Flower Mantis (*Blepharopsis mendica*)

As adult Lesser Devil's Flower Mantids transition out of the nymph stage, they transform from tan or brown to adults with beautiful markings in patterns of blue, white, and green.

Although lacking in an impressive threat display, they are still considered to be one of the most attractive mantis species, reaching a maximum adult length of 2.5 in / 6.4 cm. They are native to the Middle East and North Africa.

Giant Deadleaf Mantis (*Deroplatys desiccata*)

The Giant Deadleaf Mantis is well named, and becomes easily invisible in a mass of dead foliage. This is the largest of the "dead leaf mimics."

Adults reach a maximum length of 3.0 in / 7.6 cm or more. They feed heartily, but females rarely consume the males during mating.

Unfortunately, the species is a challenge to keep due to the overall disinterest males exhibit in breeding. The species is found in Borneo, Java, western Malaysia, Sumatra, and other parts of Southeast Asia.

Purple Boxer Mantis (*Ephestiasula pictipes*)

The fascinating Purple Boxer Mantis displays a black and white pattern on the inner femora. The species is popular with hobbyists since they can be kept communally with little cannibalism so long as care is taken with older nymphs and adults to keep them well fed.

They are known for their voracious appetites. Nymphs have purple highlighting, while adults are gray with greenish wings. The species is native to India.

Horned Boxer Mantis (*Hestiasula brunneriana*)

Small, at just under an inch when fully grown, the Horned Boxer Mantis uses its enlarged front femora to identify itself to others of its kind by waving.

The species is extremely hardy and can be successfully raised to adulthood in a 5 oz / 0.15 L cup. They are indigenous to east Asia and India.

Giant Stick Mantis (*Hererochaeta strachani*)

The long and slender Giant Stick Mantis has a knobby body that looks a bit like a branch. Females grow to a maximum size of 5.0 in / 12.7 cm. They are an interesting species, but difficult to locate outside their native range in west and central Africa.

Giant Mantis (*Hierodula membranacea*)

Adult Giant Mantids reach a maximum size of 3.5 - 4.5 in / 8.9 – 11.4 cm. The females will tackle almost any kind of insect with which they are presented.

There are 104 species of Giant Mantis, all found in China, India, Nepal, Malaysia, Sri Lanka, and other areas of Asia.

Orchid Mantis (*Hymenopus coronatus*)

The Orchid Mantis is a highly sought after species for its incredible beauty. The nymphs actually do resemble *Phalaenopsis spp.* orchids, down to exhibiting the same nectar guide markings on the dorsal abdomen.

The pink and green markings that are so lovely in the nymphs disappear in adults, replaced by brown and white. They are still highly attractive, however, and the transformation is fascinating to observe.

The species requires well-ventilated cages. The life span for females is 8 months, with males expiring at around 7 months.

The Orchid Mantis can be found in Thailand, Malaysia, Java, Indonesia, and Borneo.

Devil's Flower Mantis (*Idolomantis diabolica*)

The spectacular Devil's Flower Mantis grows to a maximum size of 4.3 in / 10.9 cm and is distinguished by the flaring projections on its body and appendages.

Although this mantis can do well in captivity, it is recommended for a more experienced hobbyist. Cloth cages and stringent monitoring of humidity are needed for successful rearing.

The species is indigenous to Africa in a range from Cameroon to southern Ethiopia and south to Mozambique.

Egyptian Pygmy Mantis (*Miomantis paykullii*)

A somewhat "classic" mantis in appearance, the Egyptian Pygmy Mantis reaches 1 - 1.5 in / 2.5 – 3.8 cm in length when fully grown. They breed easily and are an excellent species for enthusiasts new to the hobby.

While females do exhibit cannibalism, pairs can be successfully mated in just a 1.0 gal / 3.8 L container. As the name suggests, they are native to northern Africa.

Ant Mantis (*Odontomantis planiceps*)

The Ant Mantis is another excellent species for beginners. They are very "standard" in their appearance, but grow to be less than 1.0 in / 2.5 cm as adults.

Their small size allows for the use of minimal enclosures, which is useful for beginners more or less "testing" out the hobby.

In the wild, the Ant Mantis is a creature of the rain forests and gardens of India and Southeast Asia.

Zebra Mantis (*Omomantis zebrata*)

The Zebra Mantis is, as the name would suggest, one of the more unique mantis species. They are mostly green as nymphs, but become black striped as they grow.

Adults reach a maximum size of 2.5 in / 6.4 cm. The species is native to a range extending from Kenya into South Africa.

New Zealand Mantis (*Orthodera novaezealandiae*)

The New Zealand Mantis is the only mantis native to New Zealand. As adults, they are just less than 1.0 in / 2.5 cm long. Nymphs, in particular, resemble leaves.

Although a handsome and relatively hardy species, they are difficult to breed in captivity.

Tanzanian Boxer Mantis (*Otomantis scutigera*)

Adult Tanzanian Boxer Mantids are green and brown. Both males and females have full-length wings, but the males are more likely to fly.

Like most boxers, they use their enlarged and colorful front femora to signal to others of their kind, a behavior that disappears as they pass from the nymph stage to adulthood.

A good species for enthusiasts, Tazmanian Boxers often do well in captivity for up to ten generations.

African Banded Mantis (*Parasphendale affinis*)

The African Banded Mantis has curved front legs that are banded in a pattern of light and dark, with jagged "teeth" down each side. Adult females reach a maximum length of 2.5 in / 6.4 cm, with males at less than 1.5 in / 3.8 cm.

Both nymphs and adults are aggressive feeders. A once popular species with enthusiasts, they are now difficult to locate.

Ghost Mantis (*Phyllocrania paradoxa*)

The Ghost Mantis is a species with a "leaf head" that is characterized by a twisted projection. Similar lobes are present on the abdomen and walking legs.

Not only is the Ghost Mantis magnificent in its appearance, it is an easy species to keep.

Both genders reach a maximum adult size of 2 in / 5 cm. They grow slowly and have a long lifespan of 9 months. Body coloration ranges from tan to dark brown, black, and even golden yellow.

Peacock Mantis (*Pseudempusa pinnapavonis*)

The Peacock Mantis has the ability to open its wings for a magnificent threat display that looks like the markings on the feathers of a peacock. Females reach a maximum size of 3.5 in / 8.9 cm.

This species requires a large cage to avoid problems with molting. They are indigenous to the rain forests of Thailand and Burma.

Giant Indonesian Shield Mantis (*Rhombodera stalii*)

The Giant Indonesian Shield Mantis reaches a maximum length of 3.0 in / 7.6 cm. Adults are a striking and vibrant green. This is an excellent species to keep as a companion insect.

It is very rare for there to be bad molts, but the final transition to adulthood should take place in circumstances of low humidity. Females lay generous oothecae containing as many as 300 eggs.

Unicorn Mantis (Ceratomantis sausurii)

The Unicorn Mantis is a spectacular flower mantis with a prominent horn on its head and pronounced spiny bumps on the first segment of the thorax.

The antennae oscillate all the time. Females lay very thin oothecae that contain only about 15 eggs. Both males and females reach a maximum length of 1.0 in / 2.5 cm.

The Unicorn Mantis is indigenous to Borneo, South Myanmar, and Thailand.

Jeweled Flower Mantis (*Creobroter gemmatus*)

A beautiful green and tan mantis with distinctive vertical striping on the legs and a false eye pattern on the back, the Jeweled Flower Mantis reaches a maximum length of about 1.5 in / 3.8 cm

In captivity, this species will survive about nine months if provided with adequate humidity. Males can be housed communally, but females tend to be cannibalistic.

They are the smallest and most common of all the flower mantids, and are an excellent choice for hobbyists as nymphs exhibit a 90% survival rate.

Indian Flower Mantis (*Creobroter pictipennis*)

The Indian Flower Mantis is common to Asia. They reach a maximum adult length of approximately 1.5 in / 3.8 cm.

A close match to the Jeweled Flower Mantis, this species also lives approximately 9 months in captivity, needs proper humidity, and exhibits a high survival rate among nymphs.

Wide Arm Mantis (*Cilnia humeralis*)

The Wide Arm Mantis is one of the most aggressive and cannibalistic of all the mantid species when kept in captivity. They have a voracious appetite and even their appearance is threatening thanks to their oversized and wide femora.

Both males and females have rounded heads, but the females are large and very bulky. They reach almost 3.0 in / 7.6 cm in length, and produce oothecae with as many as 200 eggs. The species is indigenous to southern Africa.

Deadleaf Mantis (*Deroplatys lobata*)

The Deadleaf Mantis ranges in color from a light mottled gray to a darker gray, all intended to mimic the appearance of dead foliage. Females are 2.5 - 2.75 in / 6.35 – 6.99 cm long while males are 1.75 in / 4.44 cm.

The upper part of the thorax is shaped like a wide shield and has the appearance of a crumpled or ripped leaf. They are indigenous to Malaysia and are commonly kept in captivity.

Conehead Mantis (*Empusa pennata*)

The Conehead Mantis is found in an extended range from southwestern Europe to North Africa. It has a stick-like appearance with a long, thin body typically in shades of brown.
It is found in the wild among shrubs and herbs. A skilled flier with large wings, this species is distinct in its reliance on smell over vision for hunting.

Adults reach a maximum length of almost 4 in / 10 cm. In captivity it tends to be long-lived and is a robust choice for hobbyists.

Wandering Violin Mantis (*Gongylus gongylodes*)

The Wandering Violin Mantis does strongly resemble a violin in the curves and flares of its body. Nymphs are temperature sensitive and must be kept above 75 °F / 24 °C. They can, however, be kept together in large cages without exhibiting any significant amount of cannibalism.

Adults can reach a maximum length of 4 in / 10 cm. For the most part they must be fed flies or moths because they are ambush predators. The species is indigenous to India, Java, Malaysia, Myanmar, Sri Lanka, and Thailand.

Kenyan Banded Mantis (*Parasphendale agrionina*)

Although primarily gray, the female Kenyan Banded Mantis, when caught in the wild, can be a vibrant green.

Regardless of base color, the body is marked in pink, green, and purple patches.

The species, which is native to Kenya and Tanzania, is popular with hobbyists, and does well in captivity. Females deposit oothecae holding 100-200 eggs.

Adults reach a maximum size of 1.25 - 2.75 in /3.18 – 6.99 cm. You will also see this species referred to as the Budwing Mantis.

Yellow Orchid Mantis (*Parymenopus davisoni*)

The Yellow Orchid Mantis, though rare, is highly sought after in manticulture. As adults, these mantids are yellow or green, but they can pass through a range of spectacular color changes while maturing.

Although the species is found throughout Southeast Asia, most captive specimens are imported from Malaysia. Adults reach a maximum size of 3 inches / 7.6 cm.

Double Shield Mantis (Pnigomantis medioconstricta)

The Double Shield Mantis is hardy and large, but also one of the more aggressive mantid species. Adults can grow to 3.0 in / 7.6 cm in length and more, and are almost always gray.

After the first few instars, nymphs become highly cannibalistic. The species is easy to mate and females deposit 80-200 eggs per oothecae, but it is almost impossible to prevent consumption of the males during breeding.

The highest concentration of Double Shield Mantids in the wild is found on the island of Flores off the coast Indonesia.

Madagascan Marbled Mantis (*Polyspilota aeruginosa*)

The female Madagascan Marbled Mantis reaches a maximum adult length of 3.1 in / 7.9 cm. The species is characterized by its handsome patterning, and has proved to be hardy in captivity although a large habitat is essential.

In spite of the name, the species is found in a wide range across Africa. It is a long, slender creature with a base color of deep tan or brown.

Twig Mantis (*Popa spurca*)

The Twig Mantis has a stocky, thick build that allows it to pass as a gnarled old stick. Colorations differ by age from a light tan in nymphs to dark brown in adults. Females have short wings covering only half the abdomen, while males' wings are longer.

This species feeds well in captivity and will happily pursue large prey at the bottom of its habitat. Adults reach a maximum length of approximately 3.0 in / 7.6 cm. The Twig Mantis is native to Madagascar and sub-Saharan Africa.

Spiny Flower Mantis (*Pseudocreobotra ocellata*)

The Spiny Flower Mantis resembles many of its relatives in the genus *Creobroter*. It is, however, a much more flamboyant specimen with a heavily spined abdomen and lobed extensions on the legs.

Older nymphs and adults are marked with pink and green splashes against a white background and there is a bright, spiral shaped eye spot on the back.

Adults reach a maximum length of 1.5 in / 3.8 cm and are, on a whole, bulkier than other flower mantids. They are hardy in all stages of life, feeding well in captivity, but requiring good ventilation and adequate humidity especially during the first two instars.

The species is native to western and central Africa and is a popular choice among manticulturists.

Gambian Spotted-Eye Flower Mantis (*Pseudoharpax virescens*)

The Gambian Spotted-Eye Flower Mantis is a handsome specimen that will do well in captivity if kept at warm temperatures and misted daily. This species will reach a maximum adult size of 1.0 in / 2.5 cm.

The name derives from the two eye spots that can be found on the dorsal abdomen of adult females. The body of this mantis is primarily white, with green wings. The complex eyes form a decided point, giving the face an especially exotic appearance.

Although native to eastern, central, and western Africa, most of the examples seen in the hobby have been imported from Gambia.

African Mantis (*Sphodromantis lineola*)

Although there are 42 *Sphodromantis* species, the African Mantis, along with *Sphodromantis viridis* are the ones most commonly seen in captivity.

This is a heavy bodied mantis with a reddish brown coloration that reaches a maximum length of 3.0 in / 7.6 cm. They are fierce hunters native to sub-Saharan Africa.

In captivity, the African Mantis will readily chase prey once it has been spotted and is thus easy to keep, although communal housing is not recommended due to a high incidence of cannibalism.

Giant African Mantis (*Sphodromantis viridis*)

The Giant African Mantis is one of 42 *Sphodromantis* species. Along with the African Mantis, it is the most popular example of this group to be cultivated by hobbyists.

The species is native to western Africa, and is present as an introduced species in Spain and Israel. Individuals range in color from a dull brown to bright green and reach a maximum adult length of about 4 in / 10 cm.

Both genders have a distinct white wing spot and the inner forelegs are yellowish. The species is aggressive and displays high rates of cannibalism during mating and when kept communally.

Chapter 4 – Understanding Mantis Behavior

Cultivating an understanding of the basics of mantis behavior can offer very useful insight into the fine points of husbandry. Mantids are quite interesting in their reactions to their environment and to one another.

Common Behaviors

The following items are a major "checklist" of things you will likely see your mantis do. Some are indications of things you need to alter in their environment; others will simply help you to better understand what it is to "be" a mantis.

Be aware, however, that mantids are individuals. Even members of the same species will not always react predictably. You will be surprised, and likely delighted, by just how much personality these creatures can and do display.

Docility or Aggression

Unusual degrees of either docility or aggression can be a response to temperature. Male mantids, for instance, will become agitated, nervous, and energetic at temperatures of more than 72 °F / 22 °C. If the species is capable of flight, they'll also take to the wing.

Docile behavior can indicate injury or a health problem. A mantis that has gone too long without eating or is otherwise undernourished may simply be showing pre-death lethargy.

Failure to feed, especially in an individual that has a normally good appetite, may be an indication of physical damage to the forelegs or mouth that makes eating difficult or even impossible.

Hunger and Thirst

Hydration is an important part of mantis husbandry. You will often see a marked reaction connoting thirst. If your mantis rapidly finds and starts licking drops of water when you mist the enclosure, it is clearly thirsty and may well be dehydrated.

Hunger is often difficult to judge because many species are, by nature, much more aggressive feeders. If, however, you put prey in the enclosure and there is no reaction, you may want to remove the food insects after a few minutes, especially if there is any chance that they may harm the mantis.

Recognition and Handling

Although a mantis that is new to your collection may initially attack the hand that's feeding it — yours — they quickly become accustomed to being handled and give up on their aggressive displays

Watch your mantis, and you will realize they're watching you. This is not just the illusion of observation that is created by the dark spot in their main eyes called the "pseudopupil."

The movement of the head will clearly indicate that the little creature is tracking your movements. Some keepers swear their mantids recognize them.

Hanging Upside Down

Don't be surprised in the slightest if your mantis spends most of its time hanging upside down, generally from the lid of the enclosure. This is a perfectly normal behavior.

As unpleasant as it may sound, in many instances mantids hang upside down while feeding because the position allows all the debris from a meal to fall away from their bodies. These are very fastidious insects. They don't like to be dirty.

Constant Grooming

If you think a cat grooms a lot, you've never met a praying mantis! They groom so much, they even have body parts, like their femoral brushes, that are adapted just for grooming — in this instance cleaning the surface of the eyes.

Your mantis will also lick the spines on its legs, tend to its feet, pull down its antennae, and clean its rear legs for good measure.

Communication Displays

There are numerous ways in which mantids communicate with one another, and with things in their environment they regard as threats. The various species of boxer mantids will wave at one another with their enlarged femora.

Many species have very colorful back wings that are raised as part of elaborate courtship displays. By the same token, females that are ready to mate and broadcasting their pheromones may arch their backs.

Camouflage

Arguably camouflage is a passive behavior, but in mantids there is clearly associated intention. Mantids that mimic leaves will often contort their bodies to look more like vegetation, while bark and lichen mantids will flatten out and tuck their appendages in so as not to appear in profile.

Mantids that are elongated will hold their legs out in front of them clasped together so they look more like twigs. Many species will sway as they walk, replicating the motion of plants in the wild that will be typically ignored by potential predators.

Many species can clearly discern color as well as texture. In captivity, if provided with a choice of perches, they will settle themselves against the background that will afford the greatest degree of camouflage.

Threat and Attack Displays

When camouflage does not work and mantids are being confronted, they will either exhibit flight behaviors, which may include running, jumping, or flying if the capability is present, or engage in a threat display.

Threat displays are essentially an attempt to stand down a potential foe. While they may be more bluster than brawn, many mantids are capable of appearing quite formidable.

Often threat displays are elaborate sequences of behavior that involve raised wings, twisting of the body, and raising of the forelegs. The mantis may also turn sideways in an attempt to appear larger.

Threat displays are unique by species, and vary widely with mantids making use of colorations on their bodies or utilizing other ways of over-emphasizing their physical attributes.

When all else fails, most mantids are amazingly brave in relation to their size and will go on the attack, which may involve stabbing with the spines on the front legs and ferocious bites.

There is no poisonous species of mantis, and none is capable of biting a human with enough force to bring more than a tiny drop of blood. Basically, a mantis relies on its ability to shock an opponent long enough for an escape to be possible.

Larger species have even been known to escape the jaws of house cats by launching themselves at the surprised feline's nose causing Fluffy to back down just enough for the mantis to get away.

Can They Learn?

While most people might assume that an insect like a praying mantis will react only with natural responses that are automatic and fixed, there is every indication that mantids learn and adapt to the stimuli in their environment.

Some of their native behaviors, like choosing where they perch, where they like to molt, and how they like to feed can have a definite effect on your ability to successfully husband these unique creatures.

Since there is such an amazing variety of possible behaviors by species, it's important to learn as much as you can about any mantis you bring into your collection.

Grasping the eccentricities of any species is part of the joy and challenge of successfully raising and living with the creature, and mantids are not boring pets in this regard! They will keep you jumping!

Chapter 5 – Habitat Design and Care

As children, most of us had occasion to put a "bug" in a jar or bottle. While mantids require more than a container with a few air holes poked in the top, their habitats are still typically low-cost, do it yourself endeavors.

Pre-Made Habitats

Certainly, there are custom-made habitats available for purchase like those marketed as "Mantis Mansions" by MantisPlace.com on their website, which is certainly an invaluable resource for mantis keepers.

These items all sell for under $25 / £15 and are made of commercial grade plastic. They include 4.5 in / 11.4 cm diameter openings with custom lids that incorporate a separate feeding hole so the entire unit does not have to be removed.

This strategy lowers the chances of escape by either your mantis or their feeder insects. When not in use, the hole is sealed with a foam stopper.

Larger containers offer an option for ventilation, which is a matter of prime concern in keeping mantids and something I'll discuss in more detail later in this chapter.

Another option is to include small lights with 4-7 watt bulbs to address the heating needs of some species.

Of these containers, my favorites are the hexagonal units that are reminiscent of old-fashioned candy jars. The container can be positioned on one end so the lid is facing toward you on the side and at an angle.

The largest the company sells, at 12" x 10" / 30 x 25 cm, costs $15 / £9 plus shipping and handling. (The smallest available "hex" is 3.0" x 5.0"/ 7.6 x 12.7 cm for $7 / £4.2.)

These units would make a good "beginner's habitat," allowing you to get started quickly while generating ideas for your own "do it yourself" variations on habitat arrangements. Some people literally use plastic drink cups for hatching chambers.

Certainly, these pre-made units are superior to the ones you will see in pet stores that are often listed as "critter cages."

Not only are they made of hard plastics that offer poor ventilation, but the vent holes are too large to keep mantids or their prey contained without first screening the openings.

This may well be an option you explore as you design your own custom habitats in the future. Many a culturist spends time with a hot glue gun and microscreen working out the perfect enclosure.

As you're getting started, however, the options sold by MantisPlace are affordable, useful, and worth considering.

Other Habitat Options

As your comfort level with the hobby grows, you may find that you use a variety of enclosures for different purposes.

Some of the most common employed are recycled plastic containers, full-screen cages (also available at MantisPlace), and 10-gal / 38 L glass aquariums.

In all instances, the thing you will want to be aware of is ventilation. If you don't get good airflow in your enclosures, your mantis will simply keel over dead. Some species don't just need single vent holes, but actual cross ventilation.

The size of the container is dependent on the type of mantis you are keeping and whether or not they can be housed communally.

It may seem like madness to even consider putting potentially cannibalistic insects in one "room," but it can work fine in different life stages, if the food supply is adequate, and there's enough provided cover.

Using Planted Habitats

If you have the idea of planting an aquarium and introducing the mantids as if they are decorations, you will want to reconsider. First, mantids don't eat plants, so all you will be doing is creating an environment that may require more moisture than your pets need.

A mantis enclosure should be misted daily, but the water droplets should evaporate within 30 minutes. If they don't, you run the risk of fatal mold growth or humidity levels too high for the species in question.

A planted cage with substrate is not only going to hold moisture, but it may be more difficult to regulate in terms of temperature.

Many mantid keepers will hot glue silk flowers around the top of their pets' enclosure, both to serve as decorative elements and as a platform for molting, but eschew the use of live plants as just too much trouble.

If you do use a planted habitat, you will have to feed only flying prey insects. Other species, like crickets and burrowing cockroaches, will hide under the substrate and in the plants. This not only reduces their value as food, but it creates a danger for your mantids.

During molting, a cricket, for instance, can easily dislodge and injure a helpless mantis, and is very likely to start chewing on the poor creature in the process. You must always think about the safety of your mantids as they are developing and growing.

It's important to periodically check any corners or crevices in enclosures for simple house spiders. One spider can cause an absolute mantid apocalypse if it gets loose in a container full of young mantis nymphs.

Another consideration, although something of a "long shot" with a planted habitat is the potential for insecticide contamination. While mantids don't eat plants, their feeder insects do.

If you use plants obtained in the wild for a planted habitat, it is possible for a prey insect to ingest pesticide and pass it on to your mantis.

Look for Potential Physical Hazards

With any container that you choose, you must always be aware of potential hazards that might injure your mantis, especially when they are newly emerged from a molt.

Always look for sharp edges, and if you are using screening material, make sure there are no tiny bits of wire protruding to harm your pets. Run your fingers over every internal surface before your mantis is placed in the container and address all irregularities.

At the same time, make sure that there are no oily or greasy surfaces in the container. Such residue will prevent your mantis from climbing, which can effect where and how effectively they position themselves to molt.

Mechanics of Feeding and Watering

Regardless of the receptacle you choose as a habitat for your mantis, incorporating a feeding hole is a must. The opening should be no bigger than the neck of a large soda bottle and should be plugged with a larger piece of foam when not in use.

Typically, feeding holes are positioned at the top of the enclosure. Using a funnel, prey insects are dumped into the habitat. This method ensures that there are no escapes in either direction — on the part of your mantids or what they're getting ready to have for lunch.

If you are feeding larger flying prey, the feeding hole should be at the bottom so the feeder insects can fly up into the habitat, attracting the attention of the mantids in the process.

The feeding hole can also be used to mist the habitat, which typically is done once a day. Distilled water is recommended, since it is less likely to cause calcified spots when it dries. The water droplets from misting should evaporate in 30 minutes. If they do not, you don't have enough ventilation in your enclosure.

Regulating Humidity

The humidity needs of mantids will vary by species. This will determine whether or not you house your pets in a bare-bottomed container, or use a substrate, which can be as simple as a paper towel or as elaborate as potting soil.

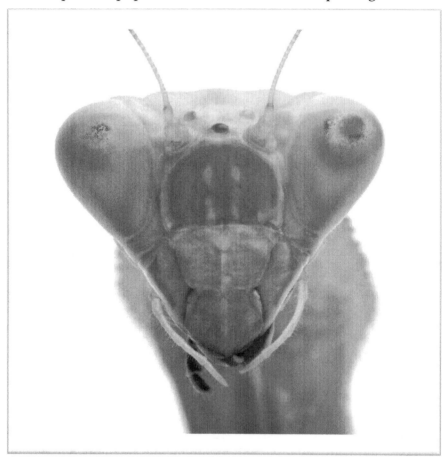

In general, however, high humidity and mantids don't go well together, just as low humidity can be extremely dangerous. This is a fine point of husbandry you will have to work out, in part, in relation to your geographic area.

In more northern regions, for instance, where home heating dries out the environment in the winter, internal humidity levels can fall as low as 5%.

In the same areas, where summer air conditioning is rare, the humidity can shoot up to the high 90 percentile during warm months.

A humidity meter will help you to understand, in a general way, the amount of moisture in the room in which your mantids are housed, but actually putting such a meter inside the enclosure doesn't give you much in the way of useful information.

The important thing to do is to watch the habitat and the inhabitants and adjust the misting schedule accordingly. If water is not evaporating in 30 minutes, mist less.

If your mantids rush to the water droplets and are obviously thirsty, mist more — and always take care to learn the needs of the specific species you are cultivating.

Considerations for Molting

In any container in which nymphs are housed, a length of metal screen or a small twig or branch should be angled from a bottom corner to the opposite top corner to provide a place for the creature to hang when it molts.

It's important that the molting surface allow a clear distance — at least 1.0 – 2.0 in / 2.5 – 5.0 cm longer than the adult length of the species in question — above the floor of the habitat.

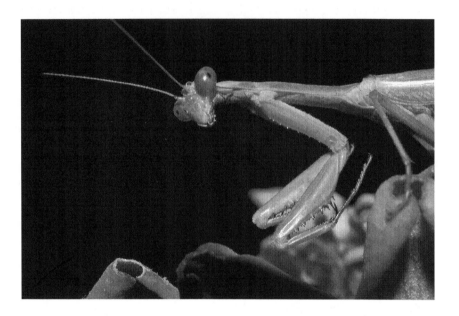

In general, minimum cage height should always be at least twice the adult length of the mantis placed inside.

Being vigilant about the distance under the molting surface will help to decrease the chance of a flawed or unsuccessful molt that can be fatal to the mantis.

In general, all small species can be housed in 5.0 -16.0 oz / 0.15 - 0.47 L containers until they reach adulthood. If a species has a maximum adult length of 2.5 in / 6.4 cm, however, they will need to be relocated to a 32 oz / 1 L container for the last few molts.

Habitat Maintenance

Mantids produce very little waste, and what they do put out consists of pelleted frass and shed exoskeletons. In the vast majority of cases, cleaning is done purely as a matter of aesthetics.

If, however, you are dealing with an environment where the ventilation is poor, or if moisture build-up could be an issue, the habitat must be cleaned after every feeding to ensure that mold and fungus do not become established.

Mantids Outdoors

It is worth mentioning that even if you do not opt to keep mantids indoors and tend their enclosures, you can still attract more of these creatures into your life by planting your yard or garden in a mantis-friendly fashion.

Various mantid species will most enjoy a setting that simulates as nearly as possible a country meadow. Allow an area that gets full sun most of the day to "grow wild."

The vegetation in this area should be both high and dense, and be especially thick close to the ground. Opt for perennials and shrubs that bloom late in the season, and include some thick evergreens.

(Late-blooming plants will provide food for your outdoor mantids just before colder weather sets in. Few insects will remain alive after October even in southern regions.)

Make certain that no insecticides are used anywhere in the yard or garden.

Buy either adult mantids or position the ootheca to establish your population. When working to build an outdoor "colony," oothecae are your best option. The large number of nymphs that will emerge will increase your chances of getting a good adult population.

Throw spoiled fruits and vegetables into the area to attract feeder insects and to act as natural fertilizer. Lights burned in the area at night will also attract other insects. (Black lights are the best choice for this purpose; just don't use yellow "bug" lights.")

Success rates will vary, and it may be necessary to restock the area each year, but during the warm months, you should see plenty of surviving mantids.

Having these creatures in your yard or garden will not only allow you the opportunity to observe, and perhaps photograph, their lives, but will also provide you with exceptional natural pest control.

Chapter 6 – Health and Breeding

There are many things a mantis enthusiast must accept before going into the hobby. You have to feed live creatures to your carnivorous mantis. Your pet will, at times, turn cannibalistic — and there will be times when you will have to euthanize creatures under your care.

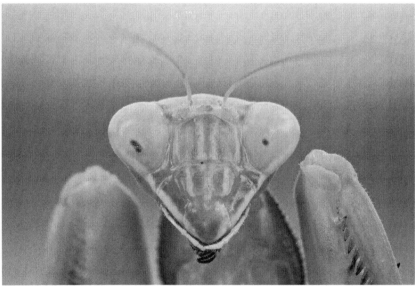

The truth is that there are almost no avenues to successfully offer medical aid to an insect. If a molt goes wrong, a method of humane euthanasia should be determined. Many hobbyists place severely damaged individuals in the freezer to end their suffering.

If you cannot accept these facts of insect husbandry, keeping praying mantids or any other insect life form is likely not for you.

Problems with Molting

A mantis in optimal position for a successful molt will be situated so that it can use gravity to assist in leaving the old exoskeleton. It is important not to try to "help" a mantis molt by pulling at the body or attempting to force the process.

(Although I have not used the term often in this book, the appropriate word to describe the phase of life in between two molts is "instar.")

Mantids' new exoskeletons are extremely soft and will tear easily. The material will also stretch, but it has no elasticity, and will not spring back in place.

It is possible for mantids to be alive after a bad molt. If the creature can still eat, it can survive, but chances are strong that it will get stuck during the next molt.

Poor hydration is generally responsible for a bad molt, but in many cases mantids will die long before they attempt to molt. In habitats with poor ventilation, mantids simply fall over dead from suffocation.

Obesity

While it may seem absurd to discuss weight issues in a species of insect, mantids, especially females, will eat to the point of engorging themselves. Although this makes them less likely to become dehydrated, obese individuals are at high risk of suffocation and will require better ventilation.

Females being fed to excess in advance of mating (a precaution taken in an attempt to keep them from eating their partners) can be seriously injured if they are dropped by accident on a hard surface.

Oddly enough, this is one case in which first aid may be possible. A small piece of paper can be super glued in place to serve as a bandage. This treatment should never be attempted with a nymph, however, since the glue will almost certainly lead to an unsuccessful subsequent molt.

Other Signs of Ill Health

The following are some of the more common "illnesses" and injuries that are seen with captive praying mantids. Almost all can be avoided by making subtle alterations in the physical nature of the habitat and the parameters of husbandry routines.

Lethargy

Any time that a mantis begins to act in an unusually lethargic fashion it is almost certainly preparing to die. Often this is caused by an overly long period of time between feedings.

Mantids will sit for long periods of time almost immobile, but will then behave with a normal amount of energy.

"Lethargy" refers to a marked and consistent change in normally observed behavior.

Damaged Tarsi

It is not uncommon for a mantid's tarsi to become damaged or broken off. The tarsus is the last segment of the legs, and the thinnest. The tarsi sometimes get caught in metal screens, or simply become brittle due to dehydration.

Malformed Wings

Malformed wings are often seen after the last molt and are also a sign of overly low humidity in the environment or a habitat that is too small. Generally, poorly formed wings are not life threatening.

Misshapen wings may, however, interfere with breeding. Some species use their wings to send signals during mating. If you are consistently seeing defective wings in your mantids on the final molt, you need to evaluate conditions in your caging arrangement.

Spots on Eyes

When brown or black spots appear on the surface of the mantid's large compound eyes, the damage is likely the result of the surface having been rubbed against the side of the habitat. This can be an indication that the mantis needs to be moved to a larger enclosure.

In nymphs, the spots may heal partially following a molt, but in adults a change in living arrangements is necessary to see any improvement. Since these spots can also be found on wild mantids, however, they are also a sign of aging and are apparently representative of pools of dried blood.

Parasites

If you acquire a wild specimen that is infested with parasites, there is virtually nothing you can do except try to prevent other individuals in your collection from being infected.

Nematodes and horsehair worms are the most commonly seen parasites afflicting mantids. Oothecae collected in the wild may be infested with wasps. You will need to confine and kill the wasps as they emerge. Depending on the timing of the infestation, some mantid eggs may still have survived.

Aging

As mantids age, you will begin to see more pronounced spotting in the eyes. Also, the body parts will turn dark or black and may begin to fall off. Many individuals vomit a tarry black substance.

Females will no longer be able to produce viable oothecae and males will not be interested in mating. Lethargy may be serious enough to warrant hand feeding to keep the elderly specimen from starving.

Breeding Considerations

Successfully encouraging mating and the hatching of fertile eggs is fundamental to the hobby of keeping mantids. Not only does successful husbandry ensure that your population remains intact, it also imparts a great deal of the satisfaction hobbyists derive from this pursuit.

Identifying Genders

Obviously it is necessary to be able to tell male and female mantids apart, but not just for the purposes of arranging their "dates." Males and females mature at a different rate. In the weeks leading up to mating, they must be housed and cared for differently.

In addition, females often turn cannibalistic during mating and bite off their partner's head. One means of avoiding this unpleasant development is to over feed the female right up to the point of mating.

Determining gender is therefore much more important than just making certain you actually have a pair capable of mating.

The most reliable way of telling the difference is to examine the abdomens of nymphs in later molting phases or instars. Look at the last segment of the abdomen as viewed from the underside of the body. You may need a magnifying glass.

On males, the last segment you can see will be very small in relation to all the other segments. On females, however, the last segment will be large and wide. In older specimens, you can also count segments. Females have five, while males typically display seven.

Timing Maturation

Males reach adulthood more rapidly and die sooner than females. In captivity, it is generally necessary to make temperature adjustments and to limit feeding in order to control the progression of molts and slow the aging process.

Female nymphs should be kept at warmer temperatures and fed more heavily, while males should be kept cooler and fed less. The earlier that gender is determined, the more accurately maturation rates can be synchronized.

You will want to take accurate notes of this process with your own mantis since these creatures are so sensitive to their surroundings. What works for one hobbyist may not work for another due to subtle and often unidentifiable differences in environment and habitat.

Another method of timing maturation is to acquire oothecae from the wild. As the nymphs emerge, mix them according to stage of development to more accurately match males and females. This generally means that the first males to hatch and the last females to hatch will be "wasted" and will have no potential mates.

Given these management considerations, it's important to keep more males and to mate multiple pairs to prevent your stock from dwindling due to unsuccessful mating. Keeping at least six viable pairs at all times is recommended, understanding that ratio includes keeping extra males.

As a general rule of thumb, males are ready to mate within two weeks of reaching adulthood. They will then be able to successfully breed for about two months before they become too old and lose interest.

Females are also ready to mate within two to three weeks. It is not always necessary to wait for a female to exhibit "calling" behavior to put the two together, however, when she begins to arch her abdomen, you can be certain that she is broadcasting her pheromones to attract prospective mates.

Pheromone Overload

In the wild, a population of mantids will be dispersed over a wider geographic area, perhaps a field, or a forest meadow.

In that setting, a female will disperse her pheromones to attract males that are flying around looking for a perspective mate. The pheromones are specialized by species to ensure that the correct message is deliver to the correct potential "boyfriend."

In captivity, however, male and female mantids live in close proximity to one another. A female's pheromones rapidly reach levels of concentration thousands of times higher than what would be typical in a natural setting. This often desensitizes the males to the point that they lose interest in breeding.

To correct this situation, it may be necessary to keep males and females in a separate area, or to increase the ventilation in the area where they are being kept together.

Managing Mating

Nymphs of both genders feed with enthusiasm and in great amount, but as males reach adulthood their intake slows to almost nothing. Cannibalism during mating certainly does occur, but in nature it is not a hard and fast conclusion that the male will be eaten.

When mating in captivity, males don't often have the room they need to get away. This is why it's important, especially if you are working with a smaller breeding enclosure, to feed the female heavily before putting the pair together.

Temperature is also an important consideration. In some species, males will not mate in temperatures of 75 °F / 24 °C and below, while others need 80 °F / 27 °C and above.

Pairing by Hand

Although hand pairing is a highly safe method, you may find that many species don't react well to this process. After the male is placed on a horizontal or vertical surface, the female is placed a few inches above or beyond him facing in the same direction.

If neither mantis moves, gently tap the female, or blow on her softly to get her to walk forward. The idea is to get the male to see and recognize the motion and begin his approach.

He will be slow and cautious, but when he sees his opportunity to jump on her back, it will be lightning fast as the poor fellow is trying to avoid losing his head!

You should have a small piece of cardboard or paper ready to be placed as a quick barrier in case the female makes a grab for the male while he's getting in position.

When the male is firmly attached, offer a feeder insect to the female. If she has something to eat, she is less likely to turn cannibalistic. The pair needs to be alone for at least an hour, so the feeding precaution is necessary.

Hopefully, when you return in an hour the male will be disengaged from the female and located at a safe distance from her.

Although this all sounds easy, it really isn't. Getting a male on a female's back is easy, but once there, he does not always mate.

If the female does not like to be handled and is dropped accidentally, she can be seriously injured. Fortunately, this is not the only approach to managing a mating pair.

Mating in Planted Habitat

Using a heavily-planted mating box (a glass aquarium with a screened lid is a good choice) can give the male mantis multiple hiding places to get away from an aggressive female.

Active feeder insects are introduced at the same time as the mating pair to keep the female well fed and distracted. The pair should be monitored for 10-15 minutes to ensure there is no immediate aggression. After that, you should leave the mantis in the enclosure for 2-8 hours.

The size of the aquarium will vary by the type of mantis being paired. If the species is large and known for its aggression, the tank should be 30 gal / 114 L or more.

The male should be removed from the habitat as soon as mating has occurred, and, if possible, a new male introduced. The second mating is a good precaution to ensure the fertility of the eggs laid by the female.

If two days have passed and you are not sure that mating has occurred, remove the male. Leaving him with the female for any longer period of time will certainly end in disaster.

Helping Males Disengage

For fairly understandable reasons, a male mantis tends to hang on to a female long after fertilization has occurred simply because he's afraid to let go!

Fertilization is at least a 30-minute process, but males have a tendency to remain where they are safest — behind the female!

If several hours have passed and the male is still in place, carefully hold the male and female by the thorax. Just the feeling of being held will give them enough stimuli to cause them to separate. Don't pull them apart. Any force will seriously injure your pets.

Managing Oothecae

The ootheca is a protective structure formed by a female mantis around her eggs to protect them from the elements and from predators before they hatch. Females may lay only a few dozen eggs, or hundreds.

Most oothecae are brown, but they may take many sizes and shapes. Some exotic species produce oothecae that are yellow, red, purple, or green. It takes only one mating for a female mantis to produce several fertile oothecae.

Supporting Mated Females

In captivity, it's often a good idea to breed the female a second time to ensure that the later ootheca will hatch. The more a mated female is fed, the larger and more viable the oothecae she is able to produce.

Be careful about the nutritional value of the feeder insects given to mated females. Good choices include the Speckled or Lobster cockroach (*Nauphoeta cinerea*), crickets, and mealworms. Stay away from inferior foods like waxworms and house flies.

Provide females with twigs and branches as egg laying sites, but prepare yourself for just how picky a female mantis can be. Some are so dissatisfied with their choices they simply dump the eggs out on the floor of the habitat. Others hold their eggs until they become "egg bound" and die.

Egg Laying Sites

Available egg laying sites should have good gripping surfaces. If a female falls while she is forming her ootheca, she won't go back to the same spot to finish the job.

Instead, she'll find a second location and rather than start over, complete the second half of the interrupted ootheca. This results in the production of a subsequent, smaller ootheca that may or may not be viable.

Working with Oothecae

Initially, the ootheca is very soft, so the egg sac should be left alone for at least 24 hours. At that point, you have two choices:

- leave the ootheca where it is and relocate the female

- remove the ootheca and glue or otherwise affix it in place in a new habitat

If you opt to move the ootheca, it must be re-attached in the same position and orientation as it was originally laid. All oothecae have a hatching zone opposite the point of attachment. This area is weaker and includes points of emergence for the hatchlings.

Generally, it is fairly easy to recognize the hatching zone as it will be of a different texture and color. If you remove and relocate the ootheca, you can reattach it with super glue applied to the "back."

Apply the glue to the surface onto which you will attach the ootheca, hold it gently in place, and then spray the exposed edges with water.

Most hobbyists hang the ootheca in a location similar to that chosen by the female initially. There is considerable debate about the best way to care for oothecae before they hatch. This applies to oothecae collected in the wild, or those that are laid by females in your care.

Orin McMonigle, in *Keeping the Praying Mantis*, suggests the following protocol:

- Twenty-four hours after the ootheca is formed, remove it from the habitat.

- Put the ootheca in a 16 oz / 0.5 L deli cup. Seal the cup and make one pinhole in the lid to ensure air exchange.

- Do not directly moisten or mist the ootheca, but put one drop of water elsewhere in the cage. If it evaporates in three days, put another drop in place. If it does not evaporate, remove the first drop.

- Date the container and wait for the ootheca to hatch.

In some instances, you may want to refrigerate the ootheca to delay the hatching of the eggs. This essentially replicates a dormant period of developmental diapause.

The eggs contained in most oothecae will still hatch if refrigerated for 1-2 months longer than they would naturally lie dormant in the cold months, but will not be viable much longer.

In general, the eggs contained in the ootheca hatch 4-6 weeks after they are deposited, or are removed from refrigerated or cold circumstances.

Do not, however, give up on the eggs in an ootheca that have not hatched, as emergence times vary widely by species and circumstance.

Always make sure there are no hazards present in any hatching container. Sticky residues and any drops of water will trap and kill hatchlings. Often, the eggs in oothecae do best when they are just left alone rather than being provided with constant care.

Chapter 7 - Feeding Your Mantids

Understand from the beginning that in order to raise healthy mantids that will reproduce reliably, you must supply your charges with living prey. Mantids are carnivorous hunters, and they're very good at it!

For the first few instars or stages of nymph development, you can give most mantid species a diet of fruit flies. In addition to eating their prey, remember that mantids can also become cannibalistic. Do not let your nymphs go hungry or they will start to eat one another!

It is always important to get a good sense of the level of aggression with any species you are keeping. Some types of mantids can be kept communally, while others are so aggressive housing them together is simply not an option.

By the second molt, most mantids are ready to move up to larger prey like young cockroaches in addition to fruit flies. You can also try to offer smaller crickets, firebrats (which are similar to silverfish), and house flies.

The Matter of Escapes

In planning your mantis habitat, you want to strive for an arrangement that not only keeps your pets contained, but also the feeder insects! The goal is always to remove the lid as little as possible.

Habitats that are sold commercially include feeding holes into which a funnel can be fitted so feeder insects can be quickly dumped inside. The hole is then plugged with an oversized bit of foam to prevent escapes.

If you are designing your own habitat, always incorporate a feeding hole, and always think about the behavior of the prey you are introducing. Mantids aren't going to go after food they can't see.

If, for instance, you are putting in winged flies, the feeding hole should be at the bottom so the motion of the flies moving up in the habitat attracts the attention of the mantis.

Size, Attitude, and Behavior of Prey

As a general rule of thumb, the larger your nymphs become, the larger the feeder insects they will both eat and enjoy. The standard measurement scheme is to provide prey that is no bigger than one third the size of the mantis itself.

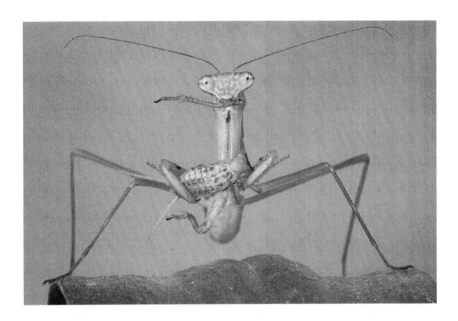

Always consider the attitude of the feeder insects in relation to your mantids. If, for instance, you are keeping a species that spends all of its time hanging in the upper regions of the habitat, you will need to feed flying prey.

Mantids that consistently remain at the top of their enclosure will likely never see mealworms or crickets that remain at the lower levels, especially if the enclosure has smooth sides that these creatures cannot climb.

Also, if you are feeding in a planted aquarium, remember that feeder insects that are not eaten right away will hide.

Not only do they not then serve as food, but they can become a hazard when given to nymphs.

Crickets can knock over and seriously damage molting nymphs or, worse yet, chew on the poor creatures while they are in a completely helpless state.

Mantid's Feeding Behavior

Mantids do not have venom therefore they cannot immobilize their prey. They rely solely on their physical strength and size to subdue and consume their prey.

Once they do, however, a mantis is not necessarily the most humane of killers. It is a myth that mantids bite off the head of the creatures they consume, thus killing them instantly.

Instead, a mantis will simply start chewing on whatever it grabs. Since the circulation system of most insects allows for massive blood loss without death, the "food" remains alive for most of the meal – struggling all the while.

The potentially squeamish hobbyist must understand and be prepared to witness this arguably gruesome sight. You are dealing with carnivores, and they will behave accordingly.

Finicky Eating

Also, understand that a mantis is perfectly capable of being a finicky eater. If you introduce a feeder insect the mantis is supposed to like, that has good movement, has high nutrition, and otherwise meets all the requirements to be a proper lunch, and your mantis just sits there? Don't waste your time again.

Nymphs will stop eating just before they are getting ready to molt, and full grown males eat very little. In general females are voracious eaters, and should definitely be "power fed" just before mating in an effort to ensure that the male survives the process.

All that being said, some mantids just don't eat much and can go a couple of weeks without eating at all. As long as the creature is not lethargic, this is usually not a cause for concern.

As I mentioned in the chapter on health, it is possible to overfeed a mantis and wind up with an obese individual. Females with engorged abdomens can be seriously injured if they are dropped, but the real danger with obesity is the potential for suffocation.

Types of Feeder Insects

Although there are a variety of insects used to feed praying mantids, the three that are most commonly selected, in large part due to their availability, are house crickets, fruit flies, and cockroaches.

House Crickets

The most common of all feeder insects is the house cricket (*Acheta domesticus*). It is sufficiently active to draw the attention of most mantids, is readily available in pet stores, and has a good nutritional value.

Fruit Flies

Fruit flies (*Drosophila melanogaster*) are typically given to young nymphs. The flies can be purchased without wings, and are even available via mail order, although they tend to be expensive.

Cockroaches

Cockroaches are typically used by truly serious hobbyists rather than an enthusiast with just one or two mantids. There are literally hundreds of species available to be used as feeder insects, and they come in a variety of sizes.

The roaches can live inside the mantid cages until your pets are ready to eat them. They do not require food and water, and they will not bother mantids that are molting.

Only one or two roaches are required for a mantid nymph in between molts if you can find specimens small enough to serve as good prey.

Other Feeder Insects

Other potential foods include mealworms, meal moths, blue bottle flies, house flies, stable flies, humpbacked flies, springtails, waxworms, and silkworms among others.

In the interest of having a ready supply of feeder insects and of keeping costs low, most enthusiasts raise their mantids' food.

If, however, you are capturing insects for your pets, be sure that the feeder insects have not been exposed to insecticides or fertilizers that will poison your mantids.

Older mantids and some especially gregarious individuals will respond to hand feeding, but other species will not respond at all to having food literally shoved in their faces. In fact, some timid species will be even less likely to eat when confronted with this kind of husbandry.

A Final Word on Feeding

Although most people do not think about this fact in the beginning, if you are going to keep mantids as pets, you are going to have to keep other insects as well — or at least be able to acquire them.

While many people have no aversion whatsoever to a praying mantis, they may well recoil in horror at a cricket or a cockroach. If you have a real aversion to other kinds of insects, this may not be the hobby for you.

The same goes for your level of tolerance with mantid's eating behavior. They are ruthless, and in their world are feared for the voracious carnivores they are.

You don't necessarily have to watch, but sooner or later, you will see your mantid tear into another living creature. If this aspect of mantid care bothers you, again — rethink your decision.

You can't make a praying mantis into a vegetarian, nor can you keep him from occasionally eating one of his own kind. Mantids are hardly "delicate" in terms of their behavior.

Chapter 8 – General Mantis Care Sheet

Please be advised that a specific care sheet can, and likely should, be written for every one of the more than 2400 kinds of mantids in the world.

If you visit enthusiast forums online, you will find many species specific care sheets. The following is an attempt to compile a generalized care sheet for the beginner contemplating entering the hobby.

In order to truly provide good husbandry for any mantis you are keeping, you must specifically research the given species.

Housing

Beyond considerations of space and design, the primary decision regarding housing must be based on the aggressiveness of the species

Not all mantids can be housed together, even if they are of the same species. Cannibalism is a major husbandry concern.

As mantids grow, they molt several times, so progressively larger habitats will be required. All must be covered, have appropriate ventilation, and an easy means of introducing food, generally via a feeding hole that can be plugged to prevent the escape of either your pet or the feeder insects.

During the nymph stage, your mantis must be provided with molting surfaces. Typically these are branches or sticks from which the mantis hangs to molt. Some species will choose to attach themselves to the lid of the habitat.

The container in which your nymphs are housed must be 2-3 times taller/longer than the full adult length of the species in order to prevent bad molts that deform the mantis.

Temperature and Humidity

Temperature may actually vary by purpose. It is possible to delay the maturation of males by lowering the temperature in their enclosure, and to stimulate mating by slightly raising it.

In general you are striving for levels that fall in the 72 – 80 °F / 22 – 27 °C range, but again, you must research by species, and purpose. The same is true for humidity.

The majority of mantid species will need their habitats to be misted daily, or regularly, but leaving a single drop of water in a hatching container may raise levels too high and create a drowning hazard for emerging nymphs.

Both temperature and humidity should be regulated, and are important elements of husbandry, but they are case and species specific.

Ventilation is also necessary since mantids can easily be subject to suffocation.

Feeding Mantids

Emerging nymphs through the first few life stages or instars will, for the most part, do well on a diet of fruit flies and similar small insects. Offer feeder insects in relation to the physical size of the nymphs you are feeding.

Increase the size and variety of the prey items as the nymphs mature. Crickets and cockroaches are both popular as feeder insects due to their widespread availability in big box pet stores and the number of sizes in which they can be purchased.

Breeding

Successfully breeding mantids is dependent on sexing individuals as early as possible. In the chapter on Health and Breeding, the process of determining sex by abdominal segments is explained.

The genders need to be separated to time the level of maturation for breeding. Males mature and die first, so their growth needs to be delayed, while the larger, more aggressive females should be power fed to reduce their chances of turning cannibalistic while breeding.

Almost all species of mantids are ready to breed within three months of becoming adults. It is not always the case that females eat the males while mating, but it certainly can happen. The chapter on breeding discusses some strategies to avoid this grisly eventuality.

In general, large cages and close supervision are recommended, as is over feeding the females and removing the males as soon as mating has occurred.

Caring for the ootheca or egg sacs is largely a matter of storing them in the correct hatching containers and leaving them alone.

Health Care

Not surprisingly, there is little that can be done for mantids if they are ill or injured. With adults, wounds can be sealed with super glue and small paper "bandages," but this will not work in nymphs as the glue will prevent a successful subsequent molt.

In instances of bad molts, if the individual is still eating, the damage may be corrected in the next molt. If this is not the case, euthanasia by freezing is the kinder option.

For elderly specimens, hand feeding can help to lengthen their lifespan, but once body parts begin to turn black, the mantid is nearing the end of its life. This varies by species, but many will survive for 12-18 months.

Afterword

If there is any negative to keeping praying mantids as pets, it's the inevitable danger of falling into the collector mentality. There are more than 2,400 species of mantids. All are fascinating, and many are breathtakingly beautiful.

It won't take you long to come up with a "dream" mantis, the one you want to keep to reach the pinnacle of your personal success story in the hobby. Be warned, however. Once you achieve the pinnacle, you'll just raise the bar a little higher!

All collectors suffer from the same disease, whether they're searching for a rare stamp or a rare mantid. For most, this constant sense of a "quest" is part of their love for their avocation.

Keeping mantids, or any kind of insect, as a companion, is a relatively new phenomenon, and one that speaks to the rapid loss of space in the modern world. For city dwellers, a more traditional pet like a dog or a cat may not be an option due to space and time constraints.

The praying mantis is certainly more forgiving in that regard, but it does have specific care requirements and like any living creature, deserves to have those needs met to the best of its keeper's ability.

Hopefully, you will come away from your reading of this text with a plan in mind — either to keep mantids for your own pleasure and education, or to appreciate them more when you encounter them in their natural setting.

Mantids are superbly well adapted for their place in the world, and well equipped to be the lordly hunters they are in the context of their domain.

Fast, efficient, and eerily intelligent, mantids look back at us with their large eyes that seem to hold both comprehension and interaction.

Certainly, mantids watch us. What they think of us, I do not pretend to understand, but the fact that in most cases they will become accustomed to handling suggests a degree of tolerance.

Regardless of your ultimate decision to keep mantids as pets or to pass on the hobby, these creatures are worth much more than a passing glance on our part. They are living testament to the wonderful diversity and creativity of nature.

Relevant Websites

Insect Lore
www.insectlore.com

Mantis Place
www.mantisplace.com

Praying Mantis Shop
www.prayingmantisshop.com

Mantis Pets
www.mantispets.com

Mantid Forum
www.mantidforum.net

National Geographic
www.animals.nationalgeographic.com/animals/bugs/praying-mantis

Praying Mantid Information
www.insected.arizona.edu/mantidinfo.htm

Nature's Control
www.naturescontrol.com/prayingmantis.html

Natural Pest Control with Praying Mantis
www.gardeninsects.com/prayingMantis.asp

Pawnation – Lifecycle Stages
www.animals.pawnation.com/stages-praying-mantis-life-cycle-6282.html

Bug Girl's Blog
www.membracid.wordpress.com/2007/08/30/its-not-illegal-to-keep-a-mantis-as-a-pet-mostly

Insect Identification
www.insectidentification.org/insect-description.asp?identification=Praying-Mantis

Bug Facts
www.bugfacts.net/praying-mantis.php#.UryLJPRDsdo

Animal Diversity Web
www.animaldiversity.ummz.umich.edu/accounts/Stagmo mantis_carolina

Ohio State University Extension Factsheet
www.ohioline.osu.edu/hyg-fact/2000/2154.html

Frequently Asked Questions

While I recommend that you read the entire text to get a better understanding of the biology and behavior of praying mantids and the requirements for their husbandry, the following are some of the most frequently asked questions I encounter about these fascinating creatures.

How long will a praying mantis live?

Maximum lifespan for a praying mantis varies by species. In general, however, you can say that the bigger specimens live longer, and that females of any species live longer than the males.

Nymphs need about 4-6 months to become adults, and will then live 3-8 months. Lifespan can be extended by keeping mantids at slightly cooler temperatures and feeding them less.

Again, however, this will vary by species. You should find out the exact temperature and diet requirements per species kept and make your husbandry decisions accordingly.

I've heard it's illegal in the United States to keep a praying mantis as a pet. Is this true?

Many states in the United States have laws against keeping a variety of exotic species. This can include tropical species of praying mantids. It is, however, legal to keep all natural and naturalized species of praying mantids found in the United States as pets.

Always abide by recommendations regarding release of any species. The prohibition against setting many exotic species loose is much more an effort to protect the hobby itself from excess regulation than a concern about the damage the mantids might cause.

This is not to say, however, that any released insect species can not overwhelm native populations. This is a serious potential problem, and one that should be avoided at all costs.

Is a praying mantis an acceptable pet for a child?

A child can successfully keep a praying mantis as a pet with the help of an adult. From the age of about 12, a young person should be able to perform all of the necessary care tasks solo.

Younger children will need help with things like temperature and humidity adjustment, feeding, and general habitat maintenance.

If a mantis won't eat, is there generally one reason why?

If the mantis is not yet an adult, it may be getting ready to molt, or shed its skin so it can reach a larger size. Mantids stop eating before they molt, and resume again after the process is finished.

If you have an adult that doesn't eat, you can try offering it different kinds of feeder insects. As long as the creature is behaving normally, there's probably no real need for concern.

Mantids can easily live two weeks without eating any food. Some species do not eat much, and males always eat less than females.

Is there any way to tell if a mantis is getting ready to molt?

A few days before the molt will occur, the mantis will stop eating and will begin to hang upside down in the cage. In some instances, a sort of white "wash" will cover the body.

Also, the area where the wing buds are located (the spot where the wings will grow in as the mantis matures) will be swollen.

Do praying mantids bite or are they otherwise harmful?

A praying mantis may well grab your finger, but only because it's mistaking you for something to eat. If the mantis is big enough, you'll feel a pin prick sensation, and you may even see a drop of blood, but that's rare.

Once you get a feel for how little the mantis is capable of biting, you won't even jump when one reaches for you.

There is no species of mantis that is poisonous, and they do not carry any diseases. All in all, it's hard to have a safer pet!

How can I tell if my mantis is fully grown?

This one is pretty simple. Adult mantids have wings, immature nymphs don't. It is true that there are some species that don't have wings as adults, but this is very rare, and typically those are not the species being kept by hobbyists because specimens are too hard to find.

You can't go by size to judge maturity. It is true that mantids grow as they age, but remember that some species never get more than 1.0 in / 2.5 cm long, while others reach as much as 4 in / 10 cm. Go by the wings. It's a much more reliable indicator of maturity.

Can I tell if an ootheca is fertilized just by looking at it?

No, there's no way to tell from the outside if an ootheca will hatch. Just treat each one as if the nymphs will emerge in time.

Females that have not been mated will still produce ootheca, but they will never hatch. This is always going to be a risk that you will run, whether your own mantids have produced the ootheca or you have collected them in the wild.

Are there any species of mantids that are particularly good for beginners?

The *Sphodromantis* species are very popular and readily available in the pet trade. These include: African Praying Mantis, African Mantis, Giant African Mantis, African Lined Mantis, Giant African Mantis, Giant African Praying Mantis, Congo Green Mantis, Common Green Mantis, and the African Mantis.

Large numbers of various *Hierodula* species from Asia are available, as are the *Rhombodera* species that are typically named the Shield, Hood, and Leaf Mantis. The Ghost mantid and Flower mantid species are also excellent for "newbies."

I've been shopping online and see that some listings for mantids include the phrase "not to be released in the US." Can you explain this?

Many of the online retailers stock exotic species that are not native to the United States. Most of those would not survive if they were released into the wild anyway, but in some warm areas like Florida and California, more hardy specimens might make it.

It is imperative for mantid enthusiasts, regardless of location, to obey legislation regarding the introduction of non-native species into the wild. It is much better to dispose of unwanted specimens by freezing them for an hour than to risk bringing the whole hobby under more stringent regulations.

I also see some species labeled "can be released in the US, but not recommended." How is that different?

The species in question are native to the United States or have been naturalized. However, most species are more common in one region as opposed to another. When release is not recommended, it's to protect native species in the area against being overwhelmed.

Most of the stock of this nature is captive bred and lack sufficient natural adaptability to survive outside a controlled environment, but again, it is imperative to obey these kinds of recommendations regarding release.

Glossary

A

abdomen - The last segment of the body of a praying mantis that is attached to the thorax and contains the reproductive organs.

adventive - A species that is not native to a given region or area but that has been naturalized.

apterous - A term indicating the absence of wings on a given species.

anterior - A term indicating the front portion of a body or object.

C

cercus - The pair of appendages that are present at the end of a praying mantid's abdomen.

coxa – The basal leg segment of an insect.

crypsis – The ability of an insect to camouflage itself against common elements in its background.

D

dessicate – Drying out due to lack of moisture and low humidity.

diapause – A period during which development becomes inactive, generally in response to adverse environmental conditions.

dimorphic - A term indicating distinct male and female shapes and characteristics within a species. The visual qualities that allow genders to be distinguished. With praying mantids the most reliable indicator is the abdominal segments.

dorsal – An upper or top surface of appendage.

E

euplantula – An adhesive pad on the tarsus or foot of a praying mantid that allows the creatures to climb smooth surfaces.

exuvium – Term describing the cast off exoskeleton of an insect nymph following a molt.

F

femoral brush – A specially adapted patch on the inner femur of a praying mantid. Used by the creature to clean the surface of the large compound eyes.

femur - In technical terms, the "thigh" of a praying mantis, indicating the segment that is located between the trochanter and tibia.

frass – Solid waste material excreted by praying mantids. Usually composed of the undigested chitin or shells of the prey insects they have consumed.

I

instar - The life stage of a nymph in between molts, designated numerically.

M

manticulturist – A term for an enthusiast who studies and keeps praying mantids as a hobby or avocation.

molting - The process by which a growing insect sheds its exoskeleton in order to gain body mass.

N

nymph - The life stage of a praying mantis in between the egg and adult stages. Since praying mantids do not undergo a full metamorphosis, there is no distinct name for the creatures at this period of their lives. Nymphs look like miniature adults.

O

oothecae - The mass of eggs produced by a female praying mantis that is encased in a protective layer of foam that hardens into a shell within 24 hours.

S

spiracle – An opening in the exoskeleton of an insect that allows air to enter a system of tracheal tubes for breathing.

T

tarsus – The "foot" of an insect, which is the last section of the leg.

tegmen – The thick front wings of a praying mantis.

thorax – The middle section of the body of an insect.

tibia – The segment of the leg of an insect that lies between the femur and the tarsus.

trachea – In an insect, an internal breathing tube that receives air from the outside via a breathing hole called a spiracle.

V

ventral – A term referring to a bottom surface or appendage.

Index

Suggestions / Reviews

I really hope you liked the book and found it useful.

A LOT of time and hard work went into writing it. I have loved these insects for years and thought it was about time I put some knowledge down on paper for others to use.

Almost certainly you purchased this book online so I'm sure you'll be contacted soon asking for your review of it by the book seller you ordered it through. I would be very, very grateful if you could provide a positive review please.

However, if you are unhappy with the book or feel I have left information out then please do get in contact first (before leaving the review) and hopefully I can help.

I'm happy to rewrite / add sections if you feel it would improve the book for other readers in the future. Simply email me via the publishers at:

Thomas@bleppublishing.com

with your suggestions and I'll get back to you as soon as I can (it may take a few days). If I can I will then act on your ideas and revise the book and send you a free copy with the updated book ASAP just as a 'thank you' for helping to improve it.

Thank you again

Thomas Green

Made in the USA
Middletown, DE
14 January 2018